a tourist's guide & a giggle..
to the
Australian 'FUNetic' slangwich

created by
Melani & Bo

special **ta** to
lynnie, ma, dad, john & the guys,
deirdre, ginny & the duke.....

a fotomoda 皇 publication

TODAY'S LITTLE BLACK BOOK OF OZ`isMs
A TOURIST'S GUIDE & A GIGGLE..
AUSTRALIAN 'FUNetic' LANGUAGE

First published in Australia in 2005 by fotomoda.

For information, write to : Melanie Lumsden-Ablan
or Roque 'Bo' Ablan III, c/- fotomoda, P.O. Box 302
Terrigal, NSW 2260 Australia.

National Library of Australia
Cataloguing-in-Publication Entry
Lumsden-Ablan, Melanie.
        Oz'isms: a tourists guide & a giggle.
        to the Australian 'FUNetic' Language.
        Includes Index.
        ISBN 0 646 45058 1
1.English language - Australia - Slang - Dictionaries.2.
English language - Australia - Slang - Humor.3.
Australianisms - Dictionaries.I. Ablan, Roque Bo, III.
II. Title.
427.99403

Cover & Illustrations by Melanie

Printed by Kenrik Australia

OZ'isms
BEFOREward

" g'day mate "

Youz all know what that means, right ?
So why, jer reckon, do youz need this
little black book ..?

Aussies speak English..don't they ?
bloody oath !.. but hang on a tick, no one's
gunna tell ya you'll need a translator...!

So, if you wanna sound like a 'tru blu
dinki di ocka' (that's a real Aussie to you) &
for those 'silly buggas' (the clowns among us)
who wanna 'av a good old 'cackle' (laugh)
or just for those of you who want a
'deadset rippa' (absolutely fabulous) little
souvenir to take home with you.....

This one's for you !

So go on, get into it & 'av a go u mug....!!

OZ`isms funetic INDEX

BEFOREward
Dictionary of WORDS

OZ`isms funetic INDEX

Dictionary of PHRASES & EXPRESSIONS

OZ`isms funetic INDEX

Word PIXS

Phrases & Expressions PIXS

oz`isms

Dictionary

of

funetic

WORDS

in

alphabetical order

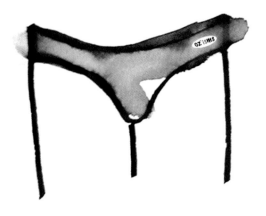

budgie smugglas

oz`isms funetic words

a gog	astounded
a looka	good looking
aggro	aggressive
ankle biter	young child
arvo	afternoon

balls up	mess up
barbie	barbeque
battla	has it tough
belt up	be quiet
bewdy	beauty
bickees	cookies
biddy	old lady
big smoke	the city
billy	tea, tea can
bindee	thorny weed
bingle	minor car accident
bloke	guy
blowie	fly
blu	fight
bludga	freeloader
bluey	redhead
bodgie	badly made

OZ`iSMS funetic words   1

B bogs	turds
bonk	to have sex
bonkas	crazy
bonza	great
boofhead	silly person
booz	alcohol
booz bus	police breath test
booz up	drink a lot
bottla	fantastic
bottlo	pub, liquor shop
box seat	best position
breakers	waves in the surf
brecky	breakfast
brewha	commotion
bricky	bricklayer
Brisvegas, Brizzi	Brisbane
brollie	umbrella
bruce	penis
bubbla	drinking fountain
budgie smugglas	men's swimwear
bugga	damn
bugalugs	what's his name
bull, bullshit	lie

OZ isMS funetic words

C

cackla	giggler
cackle	giggle, laugh
cack handed	left handed
cakie handed	left handed
canoodle	cuddling
cark it	die
chalkie	school teacher
champas	champagne
cheers	thanks, drink toast
cheesed off	annoyed
chicken	coward
chicken scratch	bad hand writing
chinwag	talk
chips	french fries
chippy	carpenter
chocka	full
chook	chicken
choppa	helicopter
choppers	false teeth
choyce	perfect
chuck up	to be sick, vomit
chunda	throw up
clobber	hit, punch

OZ`isMS funetic words

C

clod hoppers big shoes

clot	idiot
clout	influence & hit
clucky	maternal
cluey	clever
cobba	friend
cocky	arrogant
coldy	can of beer
cooee	call out
coot	difficult person
corka	a lie & really good
crack it	succeed in
cranky	grumpy
crawla	be overly nice to
creep	nasty person
crikey	oh my god
crook	sick
cross	angry
crusty	peeling
cozzie	swimsuit
cuppa	cup of tea
cut	angry
c ya	goodbye

OZ iSMS funetic words

dag	scruffy, untidy
daggy	no style
daks	trousers
damper	campfire bread
darl	darling
deadset	really
deep pockets	mean, stingy
dero	street person
devo'd	devasted
dickhead	fool
diddled	conned
digga	old man, soldier
dill	silly
dilli dally	waste time
ding	minor car damage
dingaling	silly person
dingbat	silly person
dingy	dirty
dinky di	100% Australian
dip	swim
dobba	person who tells on
dob in	inform on
dodgy	suspicious

D

dong	hit or penis
donga	penis
doonybrook	fist fight
Down Under	Australia
drover	cattle or sheep man
drongo	fool
duds	trousers
duffa	silly person
dumpa	big surf wave that knocks you down
dunno	don't know
dunny	toilet
duvalakey	when you don't know the word for the thing

E

ear bash	lecture, talk alot
egg on	encourage
elbow grease	manual labour, work at it
esky	food or drink cooler

OZ`isms funetic words

F

fags	cigarettes, gay men
fair dinkum	honest
fair go	given an opportunity
fanny	vagina & bottom
fartarse	waste time
fat cats	high income earners, wealthy people
fella	guy
fess up	confess
fizza	big build up ... small outcome
fizzy	soft drink
flabagasted	stunned
flat out	busy
flicks	movies
flog	sell
footie	football
franga	condom
freeby	no charge
fridge	refrigerator
frisky	wired, edgy
fuddy duddy	fussy
fully sick	top, great

G

ga ga	act silly over
gab	gossip
galah	silly person, fool
garbo	trash collector
gasbag	talk alot, gossip
g'day	hello
get stuffed	get lost
gimmee	give me
gizmo	object with no name
gob	mouth
gob smacked	speechless
go crook	get angry
go dutch	pay your own way
good sort	good looking
googie	egg
goss	news, gossip
grog	alcohol
grotty	dirty, grubby
grouse	great
grubby	untidy
grub	food & untidy person
gunna	going to

OZ isMS funetic words

H

hang on — wait a minute

heaps	a lot
his nibs	the boss, the top dog
home & hosed	sure thing
hoof it	by foot, walk
hostie	female flight crew
hoyfaloy	upper class
hoytee toytee	snobby
hunky dory	everything's good

I

idiot box — television

iffy	doubtful
irish mist	light showers

J

jer reckon? — do you think so?

jiffy	a moment
joe blow	ordinary person, don't know the name
journo	journalist

OZ`iSMS funetic words

K

ks	kilometer
kafuffle	commotion
kahoots	alliance
kaput	broken
kindee	playschool, pre school
kip	nap
kiwi	New Zealander
knackad	very tired
knit pick	too fussy, pick on
knocka	criticiser, put down
knock off	finish work, or steal
knuckle sandwich	punch in the mouth

L

lamington	Aussie cake
larrikin	mischievous youth
legal eagles	lawyers
lift	elevator
lip	back talk, cheeck
lippie	lipstick
lolly	candy
loo	toilet

OZ`isMS funetic words

lout	hooligan
lush	flirt & heavy drinker

maggot	dirtbag
mate	friend, unknown name
middy	medium glass of beer
milk bar	local store
mole	loose female
mongrel	canine characteristics
mozzie	mosquito
mooron	idiot
muck about	play around
muck	mess
mudguard	vehicle fender
mug	vulgar male, idiot
muggy	humid
mullet	men's hair style : short top & sides, long back
mulga	bush country
mushies	mushrooms

N

nada	nothing
nag	hassle
nagger	hassler
nanna	granny
nappy	diaper
natta	chatter
naughty	another word for sex
neither	me too, no
never never	outback country
nick off	get lost
nightie	sleepwear
ningcompoop	dimwit
ninny	idiot
nippa	kid
nippy	cold
nitwit	idiot
noggin	head & a drink
no hoper	loser
nookee	another word for sex
no worries	not a problem
nuddy	naked, nude
nucklehead	stupid
numbnuts	idiot

OZ`iSMS funetic words

O

ocka	a real Aussie
oldies	parents
on ya	good on you
oodles	lots
ooroo	good bye
orrite	o.k
outback	remote country area
oy	hey

P

paddel pop	ice cream
pardon	excuse me
pash	kiss
peckish	mildly hungry
penny pinchin'	watching your money
perks	special privileges
perve	sexually watching
pesky	irritating, annoying
petrol	gasoline
phat	cool
pinch	steal
pinnie	apron
pint	large beer glass

P

pisshead drinks a lot

pisspot	heavy drinker, a drunk
plonk	cheap wine
pluggas	thongs
pokies	poker machines
polish off	consume, finish
pollie	politician
pommy	Englishman
pong	smell, stink
poofta	homosexual
pooped	tired
pork pie	lie
porky	lie
postie	mail man
pozzie	your position
prang	minor car crash
prezzie	gift
pub	hotel
punished	smashed

Q

quack bad doctor

OZ`isMs funetic words

booz in a box

pluggas

oz`isms funetic words

R

rack off get lost

rag	newspaper
rags	mensturating
rapt	overjoyed
ratbag	rogue
ratshit	lowest level, done for
raw deal	unfair
raw prawn	try to fool you
reckie	check out a place
rego	vehicle registration
rellies	your relatives
rellos	your relatives
rigmaroll	complicated procedure
rippa	terrific
rip off	cheat, defraud
rite o	alright
ron	later on
roo	kangaroo
rooted	exhausted
root	another word for sex
rubba	eraser, condom
rubbaneck	sightseer
rubbish	trash & talk down

OZ`isms funetic words

S

sand shoes	sneakers
scallywag	mischievous person
schooner	large glass of beer
schorcha	a really hot day
screw	have sex
screwed	no chance, had it
scribble	written notes
scrub	the bush
scrubba	rough woman
scumbag	lowlife person
servo	gas station
shag	another word for sex
sheila	girl, chick
shenanigans	get up to tricks
shilly shally	too & fro
shindig	party, event
shithouse	terrible
shonky	suspect, suspicious
shout	buy the drinks
shut eye	sleep
sick	cool
sickie	day off, not really ill
skedaddle	go, get going quickly

OZ`iSMS funetic words

S

skerrick a small amount

skull	drink in one go
slack	lazy
slag	cheap woman
sloshed	drunk
slowcoach	slow
smart alec	wiseguy
smooch(a)	kiss, kisses
smoodga	charmer
smooge(e)	affectionate, cuddler
snags	sausages
sook	babylike
spag bo	spaghetti bolognese
sparky	electrician
sparrowfart	dawn
spittin'	light rain
speedo	speedometer & swimwear
spew	sick
sponge off	freeload
sport	a person
spot on	correct, exactly
spud	potato

S spunk(y)　sexy person, hot

squiz	look at
stickybeek	busy body
stiff(y)	too bad & erection
stirra	creates friction
stoked	pleased
'straya	Australia
strewth	goodness me
strides	men's long pants
stuffed	exhausted
stubby	short beer bottle
stubbies	men's shorts
stuff up	make a mistake
stunned mullet	surprised expression
sunnies	sunglasses
supa	dinner
suss	suspicious
suss out	work it out
sweetie	nice person
sweet	nice, good

T ta　thanks

OZ`iSMS funetic words

T

tat ar	so long
tazzie	Tasmania
tea	dinner
telly, teev	television
the box	television
the coathanger	Sydney harbour bridge
the goss	the news, gossip
the sticks	far out country area
thingamejig ⎫	don't know the
thingamebob ⎭	name of the thing
thongs	rubber sandals
tif	argument
tight ass	stingy
tingka	naughty
tingka	fiddle with
tinnie	lucky
tinny	can of beer
tit bits	information
togs	swimsuit
toot	toilet
tommy	tomato sauce
trannie	radio & transvestite
trollup	tart, cheap woman

T

trackiedaks	tracksuit
tru blu	genuine, for real
truckie	truck driver
trunks	swimsuit
tucka	food
tuck in	start eating
tuckshop	school canteen, shop
twerp	idiot
twit	fool
twot	idiot

U

uey	do a U turn in a car
ugh boots	sheepskin boots
undies	underpants, knickers
unit	big muscle man

V

veggies	vegetables
vegee(myt)	Aussie food spread
veg out	relax

tinny in a stubbie

aussie spread

OZ`iSMS funetic words

W

wag	skip school
wallflowa	overlooked person
wallop	hit hard
wanka	idiot
whack	hit
wharfie	dock worker
whatchamacallit?	what's the word for that?
whatsaname?	what's the name?
whatsit?	what's that thing?
westie	someone from the western suburbs
whinger	complainer
whosiwhatsit?	what's that thing?
willy nilly	any which way & wind storm
wongky	uneven
woofa	dog
woopsadaisy	oops, careful
woop woop	a remote place
woose	coward
woosie	weak person
wrapped	really pleased

yack	talk
yakka	work
yank	an American
yarn	story
yea	yes
yobbo	uncouth Aussie bloke
yongks	a long time
yooz	you
youngan'	kid, child
youz	all of you

| zilch | zero, nothing |
| zip | nothing |

2 fa	two for one
2 rite	you bet, that's right
2 ticks	in a minute

oz'isms

Dictionary

of

funetic

PHRASES

&

EXPRESSIONS

in

alphabetical order

sharks' biscuit

A

a bit toey	impatient, off
a chip off the old block	like father... like son
a hit & a giggle	fun & games
arthur or martha	uncertain
arse over tit	fall over
as if	not likely
as rough as guts	uncouth, poor job
as scarce as hen's teeth	hard to find
a tall drink of water	a tall person
av a crack	attempt
av a ganda	take a look
av a go	give it a try
av a good one	have a nice day
av a smokko	take a work break
av a squiz at	have a look at
av u lost ya marbles	are you crazy
av u got rocks in ya head?	are you stupid?
away with the fairies	spaced out
away with the pixies	zoned out
@ 6's & 7's	undecided

OZ isms phrases & expressions   29

B

back of Bourke	remote place
bananabenda	Queenslander
bark's worse than ur bite	all talk... no action
barkin' mad	really angry
bat outta hell	really fast
beetle crushers	boots
bignote u self	praise yourself
bite the bullet	accept it
bloody bastard	asshole
bloody oath	you bet
blow ya stack	lose your temper
bob's ur uncle	everythings fine
brand spankin'	new
budgie smugglas	men's swimwear
buck up	cheer up
bull @ a gate	obsessive, stubborn
bullabakanka	a far away place
bung it on	put (pile) it on
bun in the oven	pregnant
by the skin of ur teeth	just in time
by hook or by crook	whatever it takes
B.Y.O	bring your own alcohol

OZ`isMS phrases & expressions

C

call it quits   stop, give up

chalk & cheese	nothing alike
chock a block	full, stuffed
chuck a spaz	throw a tantrum
chuck a willy	get hysterical
chuck in	contribute
chuck out	throw away
cop it sweet	accept it
couldn't give a stuff	didn't care less
count ur chickens be4 they hatch	prematurely confident
crack me one	open a beer
crack it hardy	put on a good face
cut me sum slack	give me a break

D

didn't bat an eye   no reaction

did ya cum down in the last showa?   niave

dirty on	angry with
divvy up	share the proceeds
do a reckie	check a place out
do a runna	take off, leave

OZ`isMs phrases & expressions   31

D

dob in	tell on
dog's breakfast	mess
done like a dinner	well & truly beaten
don't drop me in	don't tell on me
don't know 'im from a bar of soap	a stranger
do the dirty	go behind your back
down the gurgla	down the drain
down in the dumps	to be unhappy

F

fair dinkum	honest
fart around	waste time
fed up to the back teeth	had enough
fell off the back of a truck	stolen
fess up	confess to
find a pozzie	get a postion
flappin' ya gums	talking too much
flabagasted	stunned
fly off the handle	yell & scream at
for ron	keep for later
from go to woe	start to finish
frumped out	out of shape
fully sick	top, great

G

g'day sport — male greeting

geda wriggle on	hurry up
ged ova it	forget it
ged into it	give it a go
ged on with it	hurry up
geda mongst it	have a go
get a grip	pull it together
get nicked	get lost
get off me back	leave me alone
get off me hamma	driving too close
get some shut eye	go to sleep
get stuffed	get lost
get stuck into it	start, dig in
get that down ya	eat or drink
get that inta ya	to eat or drink
get the gloves off	be honest
gift of the gab	good talker
gimme the works	food order with everything on it
give em a ring	call up, phone
give it heaps	don't hold back
go for broke	risk everything
gone belly up	all gone wrong

G

gone pear shaped went wrong

gone to the pack	rundown
goodi gum drops	yippee
got butterflies	to be nervous
got dibs on urself	big headed
got the shits	angry
got the trots	have diarrhoea
go walk about	to wander off
gud on ya	good on you
gut renching	heart breaking
guttless wonda	wimp

H

hammer & tongs full on
hard yakka hard work

haul ova the coals	get stuck into
have a chardi	drink white wine
have a dig	criticise
have a tanty	throw a tantrum
have a vommi	be sick, throw up
have sum champas	drink champagne
hell for leather	go flat out
hide nor hair	nowhere to be seen

H hit the sack   go to bed
hook, line & sinka   everything, the lot

I I'm easy   not fussed
I'm over it   that's enough

in a jiffy	in a second
in a tic	in a minute
in good nic	good condition
in the bag	a sure thing
in the drink	in the water
in the nuddy	naked, nude
in the raw	naked
in two ticks	soon
it'll be rite	it's o.k
it'll be sweet	it's fine
it'll keep	it can wait
it's pissin' down	raining heavily
it's the pits	the worst

J jer reckon? do you think so ?
jer no wot i mean? do you understand?

K

keen as mustard — very eager

keep ur mitts off	don't touch
kick in the teeth	insult
kick the bucket	die
kick up the arse	kick on the bottom
kick up a stink	make a big fuss
kit & kaboodel	the lot
knock ur block off	hit you on the head

L

lay doggo — pretending, still

legal eagles	lawyers
let sleeplin' dogs lie	leave it be
let ur head go	splurge
lickedysplit	quick smart
like death warmed up	not looking well
living the life of Riley	the good life
local rag	local newspaper
lock, stock & barrel	everything
loll about	laze around
lookamoy	look at me

M mad as a cut snake crazy

make a mug of urself	to embarrass yourself
make a quid	make a profit
make tracks	get going
me ute	my utility truck
me ol' lady	mother
me ol' man	father
muck about	mess around
mutton dressed as lamb	dressing too young for your age

N no flies on you you're sharp

no skin off my nose	doesn't worry me
not fussed	not worried
not on ur nellie	no way
not worth a bar of soap	useless
not worth a cracka	worthless
no worries	no problem
now ur cookin'	get the hang of
numbnuts	dimwit

the great Aussie

meat pie

paddel-pop

O

off d beaten track	out there
off like a bride's nightie	leave fast
off ya face	really drunk, high
on the rag	mensturating
'on ya mate	good on you
open the flood gates	let it all go
ova the moon	ecstatic
'ow ya goin'?	how are you?

P

pack a wallop	hit hard
packin' it	really scared
pack it in	give up
pain in ya pinnie	stomach ache
park ya bum	sit down
playin' possum	pretending
pillow rider	homosexual
polish off	finish
piss off	go away
pull a swifty	trick
pull ur finger out	get on with it
pull ur head in	back off, shut up
put bums on seats	to fill seats

R

rack off	get lost
raw deal	unfair
ring up	call by phone
rip or bust	no matter what
ritee o	alright
rough head	ugly
rouse on	shout at
rub it in	make you feel bad
rub ya nose in it	don't let you forget
rugrats	small child, toddlers
run amuck	go wild

S

sanga sando	sausage sandwich
shaggin' wagon	lovemobile
sharks' biscuit	boogey board
sharp as a cut snake	wise, smart
she'll be rite	it'll be fine
she'll be sweet	it'll be good
shot thru	run away
silly as a 2 bob watch	stupid
silly buggas	acting stupid

OZ`isms phrases & expressions   41

S

southerly busta	strong wind
snug as a bug in a rug	cosy
spittin' chips	furious
sponge off	freeload
spot on	exactly right
stick the boot in	kick you when you're down
stoked as	really pleased
stoked eh	really happy
strike me pink	can't believe it
stone the crows	unbelievable
stuffed up	made a mistake
swaning about	showing off
sweet as	perfect
sumthing or other	don't know the word for the thing

T

take a load off	sit down
take a sickie	take the day off
take a squiz	have a look
take the mickey	send up

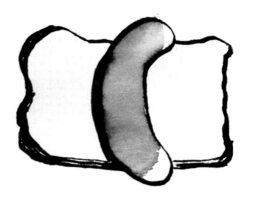

sanga sando

T

take the piss — make fun of

tear strips off ya	give you a hard time
that's a bit rich	that's harsh
that's a snack	easy
the box	the television
the goss	the news, gossip
the teev	the television
the writing's on the wall	signs are there
throw a tanty	have a tantrum
throw in the towel	give up
tight as a fish's arse	stingy
tip of the iceberg	just the begining...
tit for tat	pay back in kind
to be a fly on the wall	to watch unseen
to do the dirty	go behind your back
to leave a bad taste	not go as expected
tongue in cheek	sarcastic
tore into me	had a go at me
too rite mate	that's correct
tru blu	for real
tuck into it	start eating
turn it up	get real
turn it on	over do it, flatter

OZ`isMS phrases & expressions

u u bloody bewdy   that's great

u little rippa	fantastic
u nailed it	you did it
u shithead	you idiot
up the duff	to get pregnant
up shit creek	in big trouble
up yours	up your bum
ur bullshittin'	you're lying
ur a legend	you're great
ur a tool	you're an idiot
ur the limit	you're impossible
ur up yourself	big headed, big ego

 W water offa duck's back
doesn't worry me

waterworks	crying
were ya born in a tent?	close the door
what a hoot	what a laugh
whatchamacallit	what do you call it
whatsaname?	what's the name?
with a fine tooth comb	meticulously
woopsadaisy	to slip, be careful

W

wot ya do fura crust? what is
                                 your profession?
woodn't miss it fur quids couldn't
                                   keep me away
woodn't b dead fa quids loving life

Y

yooz all   everyone
youv got a screw loose   you're crazy
youv got buckleys   not a hope
yur off ye nan na   you're crazy

2s

2 bob short of a quid   not all there
2 pennith of God help us a total mess
2 rite   you bet
2 shakes of a lamb's tail just a minute
2 ticks   in a second

scribble pages
for your own OZ`isms

just t'get ya goin'.....

buzz off ~ go away

bee in ya bonnet ~ obsessed with

choofers ~ smokers

icing on the cake ~ added extra

keep it on the lolo ~ low profile

'on ya bike ~ get going

out of d loop ~ on the outside

same ~ agree with

toasti ~ sunburnt

*.. s'pose i don't 'av ta tell ya
dis ain't d **right** way of spelling...!*

scribble pages
for your own OZ`isms

ERIC O BRIAN

229 B METCALFE RD

RANUUI

AUCKLAND N.Z

OZ`isms scribble pages

scribble pages
for your own oz`isms

----

oz`isms
AFTER ward

Could gab on bout the hard yakka put into this, but i'd be tellin' ya a pork-pie.

So i'll give it to ya fair dinkum...

All these bloody whatchamacallits ... oz`isms, came from me mates & rellos & every Joe Blow, sheila & bloke i ever met in our land down under ..

So ta to all you ockas across this big brown land of oz ..!

Youz all know who youz r ....sweet !

c ya ......

ps. Oh yea, i left ya some scribble pages
for your own chicken scratch ....
just in case i've missed a few oz`isms.